The Zuni

by Petra Press

Content Adviser: Dr. Bruce Bernstein, Assistant Director for Cultural
Resources, National Museum of the American Indian, Smithsonian Institution

Social Science Adviser: Professor Sherry L. Field,
Department of Curriculum and Instruction, College of Education,
The University of Texas at Austin

Reading Adviser: Dr. Linda D. Labbo,
Department of Reading Education, College of Education,
The University of Georgia

COMPASS POINT BOOKS

Minneapolis, Minnesota

Compass Point Books
3722 West 50th Street, #115
Minneapolis, MN 55410

Visit Compass Point Books on the Internet at *www.compasspointbooks.com* or e-mail your request
to *custserv@compasspointbooks.com*

Cover: A Zuni squash blossom necklace

Photographs ©: Marilyn "Angel" Wynn, cover, 13, 43; N. Carter/North Wind Picture Archives, 4,
15; Denver Public Library/Western History Collection, 5, 14, 26–27, 37; Hulton Getty/Archive
Photos, 8; North Wind Picture Archives, 9, 18, 20, 22, 24, 29, 30, 34, 38; Kent & Donna Dannen,
10, 17, 21, 39; National Museum of American Art, Washington, D.C./Art Resource, N.Y., 11,
32–33; Courtesy Museum of New Mexico, photo by Ben Wittick, neg. #58849, 12; Bettmann/
Corbis, 16; AP/Wide World Photos, 19; David & Peter Turnley/Corbis, 23; Courtesy Museum of
New Mexico, neg. #68770, 25; Dave G. Houser/Corbis, 28; Courtesy Museum of New Mexico,
photo by John K. Hillers, neg. #29893, 31; Stock Montage, 35; Courtesy Museum of New Mexico,
photo by G. Wharton James, neg. #107770, 36; Tom Bean/Corbis, 40–41; Reuters NewMedia
Inc./Corbis, 42.

Editors: E. Russell Primm, Emily J. Dolbear, and Alice K. Flanagan
Photo Researchers: Svetlana Zhurkina and Jo Miller
Photo Selector: Catherine Neitge
Designer: Bradfordesign, Inc.
Cartographer: XNR Productions, Inc.

Library of Congress Cataloging-in-Publication Data
Press, Petra.
   The Zuni / by Petra Press.
      p. cm. — (First reports)
   Includes bibliographical references and index.
   ISBN 0-7565-0189-X
   1. Zuni Indians—Juvenile literature. [1. Zuni Indians. 2. Indians of North America—New
Mexico] I. Title. II. Series.
E99.Z9 P74 2002
978.9004'979—dc21   2001004413

Table of Contents

An Ancient People 4

Zuni Villages 10

Desert Farming 14

The Way of the Spirits 18

The Spanish Missions 21

Fighting the Spanish 25

A New Way to Live 28

Rebuilding a Homeland 32

Protecting the Land 37

Zuni Life Today 40

Glossary 44

Did You Know? 45

At a Glance 45

Important Dates 46

Want to Know More? 47

Index 48

An Ancient People

▲ *Zuni rain dancers perform in Gallup, New Mexico.*

The Zuni (pronounced ZOO-nee) people have a long history. They have been living in the deserts of the southwestern United States for thousands of years.

The Zuni are one of nineteen Native American groups known as the Pueblo Indians. *Pueblo* is a Spanish word that means "village." Explorers called the Indian villages **pueblos** because they looked like Spanish towns. They also called the Indians who lived in these villages the Pueblo.

The Zuni call themselves *Ashiwi*. This word means "the flesh" or "belonging to the Zuni people." They

▲ *A late nineteenth century photograph of dancers in Zuni dress*

▲ The Zuni homelands and reservation

share history and traditions with other Pueblo Indians. The Zuni speak a different language, however. They also have their own beliefs.

Today, most Zuni live in northwestern New Mexico in or near the village called Zuni Pueblo. In the past, the Zuni lived in parts of what is now Colorado, Utah, and Arizona.

Many people believe the Zuni are related to an ancient people called the Mogollon. These people lived in caves in New Mexico, Arizona, and northern Mexico thousands of years ago. They moved from place to place. They hunted animals and gathered food.

Then the Mogollon began to settle down to grow crops. They built villages near their fields. The first crop they grew was corn. The people also learned to grow beans and squash. Corn, beans, and squash are still an important part of the Zuni diet.

The Mogollon's first houses were called pit houses. These log houses were covered with branches, reeds, and mud. The floors were dug about 3 feet (1 meter) below the ground.

Later, the Mogollon made stone houses covered with a plaster of mud and straw. They built one house on top of the other. Ladders connected the houses. Several related families shared rooms.

▲ *The Mogollon made thousands of rock drawings at Three Rivers in southern New Mexico.*

▲ *Anasazi ruins of Pueblo Bonito in Chaco Canyon in New Mexico*

As the Mogollon traveled, they saw how other people lived. They learned from early Pueblo Indians called the Anasazi. The Mogollon built houses under rocky cliffs, as the Anasazi people did.

Today, you can visit the ruins of some of these ancient houses. You can see them at Chaco Culture National Historical Park and the Bandelier National Monument in New Mexico.

Zuni Villages

The first Zuni village, or pueblo, was called Halona. Six other villages were built in the valley along the Zuni River in New Mexico. Later, for protection, they built villages on flat-topped hills called **mesas**.

▲ *Corn Mountain is a sacred Zuni place.*

▲ *A street in Zuni Pueblo in an 1888 painting*

The pueblos were comfortable to live in. The rooms were built on top of each other. The Zuni used ladders or stone stairs to get to the different levels.

Houses on the first floor had no windows or doors. People climbed down a ladder through a hole in the roof.

Inside the buildings, rooms were in long rows. Parents and their children lived together. Related families lived next to one another.

Families were grouped in **clans**. Each clan was named for something in nature. Eagle, Deer, Corn, Water, and Sun are some clan names. Today, many Zuni families have the same names.

▲ *The inside of a house in Zuni Pueblo in an 1895 photograph*

▲ *Zuni women perform an ancient pottery dance in Gallup, New Mexico.*

Zuni mothers passed on the family name and goods to the children. A married couple lived with or near the wife's family. Children were born into the mother's clan. If a couple divorced, children stayed with their mother.

Desert Farming

▲ *Zuni gardeners tend to their plants at Hawikuh in this photograph from the early twentieth century.*

Growing food was an important activity in Zuni villages. Each family was in charge of a piece of land. Everyone had to work together. It took great skill to grow crops in such dry land.

▲ *The Zuni planted corn, beans, and squash together.*

The Zuni men got the fields ready for planting. They dug ditches from the river to water their fields. Then, they planted corn, beans, and squash. Then they protected the growing crops from hungry animals.

When the crops were ready to be picked, everyone helped gather them. They stored enough food to get through the winter.

Men also hunted deer, sheep, rabbit, and bear in the mountains. They caught beavers, squirrels, and field mice along the rivers. They fished and set traps for wild ducks.

▲ *A Zuni woman grinds corn in the early twentieth century.*

Women prepared the food. They often cooked with corn. They boiled, roasted, or crushed corn into a coarse powder called cornmeal. Women made mush, bread, or tortillas from the cornmeal. Crushing corn, nuts, and seeds with a stone took a lot of time.

Meat was eaten roasted or boiled. It was also cut into strips and dried in the sun to eat later.

Women also cooked with onions, wild grains, and wild potatoes. They flavored them with nuts, berries, and fruits. Some of these old recipes are still popular among the Zuni today.

▲ *Outdoor ovens are used to bake bread at Zuni Pueblo.*

The Way of the Spirits

The Zuni believe that everything in life has a soul or spirit within it. Plants, animals, the sun, and the rain have spirits. Spirits also live in things made by people, such as pottery and masks.

The most important spirits are Mother Earth and Father Sky. Mother Earth gives and feeds life. Father Sky provides the sun and rain that Mother Earth needs.

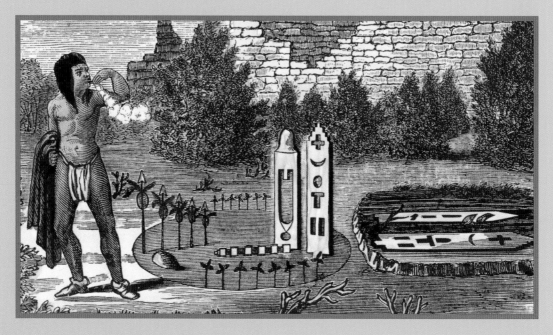

▲ *A Zuni altar*

▲ *A Zuni boy performs the traditional turkey dance.*

The Zuni pray often to the spirits. They may ask for a long life, healthy children, courage, or understanding. Or they may ask for good weather, rain, or crops.

The Zuni hold **ceremonies** to honor and thank the spirits. Some ceremonies are performed in underground buildings called **kivas**.

During the ceremonies, the Zuni dance and sing. There are war dances, animal dances, and dances during the planting season. Some dances honor Christmas, Easter, and All Souls' Day.

▲ *The Shalako ceremony*

An important ceremony called the Shalako is held each year in late November or early December. During the ceremony, the Zuni welcome spirits into the pueblo. Those spirits are called **kachinas**. The Zuni ask the kachinas for their blessings.

Some clan members paint their bodies and wear masks to look like the kachinas. Then they dance and sing.

The Spanish Missions

In 1540, a Spanish explorer named Francisco Vásquez de Coronado arrived in the Zuni territory. He came with soldiers and Catholic **missionaries**. They wanted to find gold and claim land for the king of Spain.

▲ *Spanish explorers, as well as Indians and pioneers, carved their names in a huge rock at El Morro National Monument near Zuni Pueblo.*

▲ The rock at El Morro National Monument where a Spanish explorer, Juan de Oñate, carved his name in 1605

The Spanish had heard stories about cities made of gold. They called these cities the Seven Cities of Cíbola. Coronado thought the Zuni villages might be the famous Cities of Cíbola. He found only farming communities, however.

The Spanish took control of the Zuni villages anyway. The Zuni fought the soldiers, but the Spanish had better weapons.

In time, the Spanish renamed the Zuni villages. They forced the Zuni to build Spanish farms and churches. The missionaries called these Spanish villages **missions**. The first Spanish mission was built in the Zuni village of Hawikuh in 1629.

▲ *Zuni artist Alex Seotewa stands in front of a Spanish mission in Zuni Pueblo that was built in 1629.*

▲ *The Flying Eagle Man,*
war god of the Zuni

The missionaries wanted the Zuni to become Christians. They punished them for practicing their own religion. The Zuni would not give up their beliefs.

The Spanish ruled the Pueblo Indians harshly for the next 140 years. They treated them as slaves. They made the Indians pay high taxes.

Many Pueblo Indians were killed by European illnesses such as measles and smallpox. Often, enemy tribes looking for food attacked their villages. Then a long, dry spell wiped out their crops and killed their animals. All the Pueblo Indians suffered during this difficult time.

Fighting the Spanish

Around 1670, many Pueblo Indians began to practice their religion openly. They believed that returning to their old ways would make life better.

Then the Spanish arrested Indians who took part in kachina dances. They even put four religious leaders

▲ *A man makes a kachina doll at Zuni Pueblo in this photograph from the late nineteenth century.*

to death. In 1680, secret meetings were held in every pueblo. Runners went from village to village carrying messages.

A man named Popé took charge. He and others made plans to go against Spanish rule. They decided to drive the Spanish out of their land.

In August 1680, the Zuni and other Pueblo Indians fought back. They killed missionaries. They burned down churches.

At the time, the Zuni were living in only three pueblos—Halona, Matsaki, and Kiakima. When the fighting began, most people left the villages. They fled to Towayalane, or Corn Mountain. The fighting lasted several days. Finally, the last group of Spanish left.

For the next twelve years, the Pueblo Indians were again in control of their land. Popé became governor of all the pueblos. He ruled just as harshly as the Spanish.

When Popé died in 1688, the Spanish returned to the Southwest. They began taking back the pueblos.

▲ A photograph of Corn Mountain and Zuni Pueblo in the late nineteenth century

A New Way to Live

▲ *Zuni dancers at the Indian Pueblo Cultural Center in Albuquerque, New Mexico*

One by one, the pueblos fell to the Spanish. By 1692, most of the pueblos were once again under Spanish rule.

Around 1699, the Zuni were forced to come down from Corn Mountain. They agreed to stop fighting the Spanish. The Zuni never agreed to give up their religion. They said they must govern themselves.

▲ *The Zuni raised sheep.*

In time, the Zuni and the Spanish began to get along with one another. Sometimes they even fought together against the Navajo and Apache.

The Zuni learned many new things from the Spanish. They learned how to grow wheat, oats, peaches, and toma-toes. They also raised small donkeys called burros and sheep. The animals provided the Zuni with transportation, meat, and wool for weaving. Metal tools such as axes, saws, scissors, and knives made their lives easier, too.

Spanish rule over the Southwest ended in 1821. At that time, Spain lost a war with Mexico. They had to give up Pueblo lands. Control of the Pueblo Indians passed from Spain to Mexico.

The Mexican government let the Pueblo Indians become citizens. They did not force their way of life on the Native Americans. Pueblo lands were part of Mexico until 1848.

▲ *The United States gained control of the Southwest after it beat Mexico in a war in 1848.*

▲ *This 1880 photograph shows a house at Zuni Pueblo.*

In 1848, Mexico and the United States ended the Mexican War. They signed the **Treaty** of Guadalupe-Hidalgo. It gave the United States the Southwest, including Pueblo lands.

In return, the U.S. government promised to protect Pueblo Indian property and religion. Everyone could become U.S. citizens. The Pueblo Indians were the only Native North Americans to become U.S. citizens in this way.

Rebuilding a Homeland

Each time a new country took control, the Zuni had to rebuild their homeland. The Zuni believed that

the Treaty of Guadalupe-Hidalgo would protect their rights.

However, in 1848, gold was discovered in California. Thousands of gold seekers crossed Zuni lands to get to California. Along the way, these people stole Zuni crops and animals.

Some people even built homes on Zuni land. They settled down and began to farm or log. Others came to mine **uranium** in the area. Then missionaries came to spread the Christian religion.

◄ *California miners in an 1852 oil painting*

▲ Building a railroad brought more and more people to Zuni lands.

Soldiers came to protect everyone. Before long, the U.S. government built forts for the soldiers, and settlers built towns.

▲ *President Rutherford B. Hayes*

Soon the railroad came through. Traders bought Zuni sheep and cattle and shipped them to cities all over the United States. Trade was good, but the Zuni were losing too much of their land to outsiders.

The Zuni asked the U.S. government to honor the Treaty of Guadalupe-Hidalgo. They asked the government to protect their rights to the land.

The U.S. government had no exact measurement of Zuni lands on file. In 1877, President Rutherford B. Hayes had a **survey** done.

▲ *Zuni gardens in the late nineteenth century*

The U.S. survey reduced the Zuni territory to one-tenth of its original size! Once again, the Zuni had lost land.

Protecting the Land

In 1924, the U.S. Congress passed the Pueblo Lands Act. This law is still in force today. It says that people cannot settle on Pueblo land without permission.

After the Pueblo Indians finally had a law to protect their land, life improved. Slowly, the Zuni population grew.

▲ *Zuni Pueblo in the 1920s, when the U.S. Congress passed the Pueblo Lands Act*

In the 1950s, many young people began to work outside their villages. They found jobs on the railroad and in nearby towns, vineyards, and mines. On the weekends, they returned home to their pueblos.

Many older Zuni continued to farm the land in the old ways. Today, new and old ways exist side by side in the Zuni villages.

▲ Cornfields near Zuni Pueblo

▲ *The desert near Zuni Pueblo*

Some Zuni leaders belong to an organization for Pueblo Indians. It protects their interests, land, and water. It is called the All-Pueblo Council.

In 1990, the U.S. Congress passed the Zuni Land Conservation Act. This law prevents mining and timber companies from building on Zuni land.

The Zuni are proud of their customs and beliefs. They have a strong sense of family and community. Few Native Americans have held on to the old ways as well as the Zuni have.

Yet the Zuni take part in modern American life also. A large number of Zuni youth go to college. Many Zuni people speak three languages—Zuni, Spanish, and English.

◄ *Zuni girls wear traditional dance costumes and jewelry for a festival in Arizona.*

▲ *Zuni fire fighters at work near Los Alamos, New Mexico*

Zuni people work in many fields. They are lawyers, teachers, and computer specialists. In the pueblos, many Zuni raise livestock or work on nearby farms. Some serve as fire fighters for the U.S. Forest Service.

Many Zuni are skilled artists. They sell their weavings, drums, pottery made from local clay, and kachina dolls. They also carve masks and small figures out of wood and stone. Zuni artists are known for their silver and **turquoise** jewelry.

From ancient times, the Zuni have lived in a difficult land. They know the importance of respecting nature and working with others. These lessons have made them who they are today as Zuni and as Americans.

▲ *The Zuni are well known for their small carvings.*

Glossary

ceremonies—formal actions to mark important times

clans—groups of families living together

kachinas—Pueblo Indian spirits

kivas—underground buildings where special ceremonies take place

mesas—flat-topped hills

missionaries—people who travel to foreign countries to spread their religion

missions—a church or other place where missionaries live and work

pueblos—villages of clay and stone buildings built by Native American tribes in the southwestern United States

survey—the process of measuring for size, shape, position, or boundaries

treaty—an agreement between two governments

turquoise—a clear blue or greenish blue gemstone mined in the southwestern United States

uranium—a white metal that is the main source of nuclear energy

Did You Know?

- In the past, the most important people in Zuni villages were the rain priests. They prayed to the spirits who brought rain.

- The Zuni raised turkeys for their feathers. They ate turkeys only when other food was in short supply.

- Zuni children are taught by encouragement and example, not by punishment. However, they are told scary stories about kachinas who carry off naughty children and eat them.

At a Glance

Tribal name: Zuni

Past locations: Colorado, Utah, Arizona

Present location: New Mexico

Traditional houses: Pit houses, cliff dwellings, multifamily clay and stone buildings

Traditional clothing materials: Skins, woven cotton

Traditional transportation: Foot, burros

Traditional food: Corn, beans, squash, meat, fish, wild plants

Important Dates

500 B.C.	The Mogollon live in the southwestern United States.
1000	The Zuni begin living in the pueblo village of Zuni.
1540	Spanish explorer Francisco Vásquez de Coronado arrives in Zuni territory.
1629	The first Spanish mission is built at the Zuni village of Hawikuh.
1680	The Zuni and other Pueblo Indians drive the Spanish from their land.
1692	Pueblo Indian villages are once again under Spanish rule.
1821	Control of Pueblo Indian lands passes from Spain to Mexico.
1848	The Mexican War ends and the Treaty of Guadalupe-Hidalgo is signed.
1877	President Rutherford B. Hayes cuts the Zuni territory to one-tenth of its original size.
1924	The U.S. Congress passes the Pueblo Lands Act.
1990	The U.S. Congress passes the Zuni Land Conservation Act.

Want to Know More?

At the Library

Bassman, Theda. *Treasures of the Zuni*. Flagstaff, Ariz.: Northland Pub., 1996.

Doherty, Katherine M. *The Zuni*. New York: Franklin Watts, 1993.

Flanagan, Alice K. *The Zuni*. Danbury, Conn.: Children's Press, 1998.

On the Web

The North American Indian: The Zuni

http://www.curtis-collection.com/tribe%20data/zuni.html

For essays and photographs by historian Edward Sheriff Curtis

The Zuni at the Dallas Museum of Art

http://pw1.netcom.com/~wandaron/zuni.html

For information about Zuni art, literature, traditions, and religious practices

Through the Mail

Pueblo of Zuni

P.O. Box 339

Zuni, NM 87327

To find out more about the history and traditions of the Zuni

On the Road

Bandelier National Monument

Los Alamos, NM 87544

505/672-0343

To see the remains of ancient Pueblo communities

Index

Anasazi Indians, 9
Apache Indians, 29
art, 43
beans, 7, 15
burros, 29
ceremonies, 19
children, 13
clans, 12
corn, 7, 15, 16
Corn Mountain, 26, 28
de Coronado, Francisco Vásquez, 21
dance, 19, 20
disease, 24
divorce, 13
education, 41
families, 12, 13, 41
fishing, 15
gold, 22, 33
government, 27, 28, 39
Halona Pueblo, 10, 26
Hawikuh Pueblo, 23
Hayes, Rutherford B., 35
houses, 8, 9, 11
hunting, 7, 15
kachinas, 20, 25

Kiakima Pueblo, 26
kivas, 19
language, 5, 7, 41
marriage, 13
Matsaki Pueblo, 26
men, 15
Mexican War, 31
missions, 23
Mogollon people, 7–9
names, 12
Navajo Indians, 29
pit houses, 8
Popé, 26, 27
Pueblo Indians, 5, 7
Shalako ceremony, 20
slavery, 24
squash, 7, 15
trapping, 15
Treaty of Guadalupe-Hidalgo, 31, 33, 35
turquoise, 43
uranium mining, 33
women, 13, 16, 17
Zuni Pueblo, 7
Zuni River, 10

About the Author

Petra Press is a freelance writer of young adult nonfiction, specializing in the diverse culture of the Americas. Her more than twenty books include histories of U.S. immigration, education, and settlement of the West, as well as portraits of numerous original cultures. She lives with her husband, David, in Milwaukee, Wisconsin.